THE

# STORY OF RIMINI,

## A POEM,

BY

# LEIGH HUNT.

THIRD EDITION.

1819.

British Library Cataloguing-in-Publication Data
A catalogue record for this book is available from the
British Library

# Leigh Hunt

James Henry Leigh Hunt – better-known by his pen name, Leigh Hunt – was born in London, England in 1784. He was educated at Christ's Hospital, entering the school shortly after Samuel Taylor Coleridge and Charles Lamb had both left. Hunt published his first volume of poetry, *Juvenilia* (1801), at the age of just seventeen, and for the rest of his life was immersed in the literary and theatrical worlds.

Hunt began to write for the newspapers, and in 1807 published a volume of theatre criticism. From 1808 onwards, he worked for the *Examiner,* a popular and often vitriolic paper which earned Hunt a two-year stint in prison for an attack he penned on the Prince Regent. Upon his release form prison, he spent a year editing *The Reflector,* before focussing again on his poetry. In 1816, he published his most significant work, *Story of Rimini,* and followed this with *Foliage* (1818), *Hero and Leander* (1819) and *Bacchies and Ariadne* (1819). Together, these works established him as a talented and important poet.

Hunt's newfound literary fame saw him make the acquaintance of John Keats, Percy Shelley and others. However, he gradually fell into deep financial trouble. His newspaper, *The Examiner,* folded, and he troubled to make ends meet. For the rest of his life, he struggled with poverty and sickness. In spite of this, Hunt did produce some of his best poems during the 1830s, including *Captain Sword and Captain Pen* (1835). He died in 1859, aged 74.

TO

THE RIGHT HONOURABLE

# LORD BYRON.

---

MY DEAR BYRON,

      You see what you have brought yourself to by liking my verses. It is taking you unawares, I allow; but you yourself have set example now-a-days of poet's dedicating to poet; and it is under that nobler title, as well as the still nobler one of friend, that I now address you.

I shall be thought indeed by some to write a very singular dedication, when I say that I should not have written it you at all, had I not thought the poem capable of standing on its own ground. I am far from insensible of your approbation of it, as you well know, and as your readers will easily

a

imagine; but I have an ambition, at the same time, to have credit given me for a proper spirit; and in fact, as I should be dissatisfied with my poetry without the one, I should never have thought my friendship worth your acceptance without the other.

Having thus,—with sufficient care, I am afraid, —vindicated my fellow-dignity, and put on my laurel in meeting you publicly, I take it off again with a still greater regard for those unceremonious and unpretending humanities of private intercourse, of which you know so handsomely how to set the example; and professing to be nothing more, in that sphere, than a hearty admirer of what is generous, and enjoyer of what is frank and social, am, with great truth,

My dear BYRON,

affectionately yours,

*Hampstead,*                    LEIGH HUNT.
*January* 29, 1816.

# PREFACE.

THE following story is founded on a passage in
Dante, the substance of which is contained in the
concluding paragraph of the third canto. For
the rest of the incidents, generally speaking, the
praise or blame remains with myself. The passage
in question—the episode of Paulo and Francesca—
has long been admired by the readers of Italian
poetry, and is indeed the most cordial and refresh-
ing one in the whole of that singular poem the
Inferno, which some call a satire, and some an
epic, and which, I confess, has always appeared

to me a kind of sublime night-mare. We even
lose sight of the place, in which the saturnine
poet, according to his summary way of disposing
both of friends and enemies, has thought proper
to put the sufferers; and see the whole melan-
choly absurdity of his theology, in spite of itself,
falling to nothing before one genuine impulse of
the affections.

The interest of the passage is greatly increased
by its being founded on acknowledged matter of
fact. Even the particular circumstance which
Dante describes as having hastened the fall of the
lovers,—the perusal of Launcelot of the Lake,—
is most likely a true anecdote; for he himself, not
long after the event, was living at the court of
Guido Novello da Polenta, the heroine's father;
and indeed the very circumstance of his having
related it at all, considering its nature, is a warrant
of its authenticity.

The commentators differ in their accounts of the rest of the story; but all agree that the lady was in some measure beguiled into the match with the elder Malatesta,—Boccaccio says, by being shewn the younger brother once, as he passed over a square, and told that that was her intended husband. I have accordingly turned this artifice to account, though in a different manner. I have also omitted the lameness attributed to the husband; and of two different names by which he is called, Giovanni and Launcelot. have chosen the former, as not interfering with the hero's appellation, whose story the lovers were reading.

The Italians have been very fond of this little piece of private history, and I used to wonder that I could meet with it in none of the books of novels, for which they have been so famous; till I reflected, that it was perhaps owing to the nature of the books themselves, which such a story

might have been no means of recommending.
The historians of Ravenna, however, have taken
care to record it; and besides Dante's episode, it
is alluded to by Petrarch and by Tassoni.   The
former mentions the lovers among his examples
of calamitous passion, in the Trionfo d'Amore,
cap. 3.  Tassoni, in his tragi-comic war, intro-
duces Paulo Malatesta, as leading the troops of
Rimini; and paints him in a very lively manner,
as contemplating, while he rides, a golden sword-
chain, which Francesca had given him, and which
he addresses with melancholy enthusiasm as he
goes.  See the Secchia Rapita: canto 5. st. 43. &c.
and canto 7. st. 29. &c.

The romance of Launcelot of the Lake, upon
the perusal of which the principal incident turns,
is little known at present, but was a great favorite
all over Europe, up to a late period.  Chaucer,
no long time after the event itself, mentions it, in

his significant way, as a work held in great esti-
mation by the ladies. The Nun's Priest, speaking
of the tale of the Cock and the Fox, which he is
relating, says to his hearers,

" This story is al so trewe, I undertake,
" As is the book of Launcelot du Lake,
" That women holde in ful gret reverence."
*Canterbury Tales: V.* 15147.

The great father of our poetry, by the way, is
a little ungrateful with his jokes upon chivalrous
stories, of which he has left such noble specimens
in the Palamon and Arcite, and in the unfinished
story of Cambuscan, which Milton delighted to
remember; but both he and the Italian poets ap-
pear to have laughed at them occasionally, as
lovers affect to do at their mistresses. I have in
my possession an imperfect copy of Launcelot of
the Lake in Italian, and have taken occasion of
my story, to give an abstract of the beginning of

it, which appears to me as fine as any thing in
Amadis de Gaul or Tristan de Leonois.

There are no notes to the present poem. I have
done my best, as every writer should, to be true
to costume and manners, to time and place; and
if the reader understands me as he goes, and feels
touched where I am most ambitious he should
be, I can be content that he shall miss an occa-
sional nicety or so in other matters, and not be
quite sensible of the mighty extent of my in-
formation. If the poem reach posterity, curiosity
may find commentators enough for it, and the
sanction of time give interest to whatever they
may trace after me. If the case be otherwise, to
write notes is only to shew to how little purpose
has been one's reading. I shall merely observe,
that of the direct obligations, of which I am con-
scious, and which perhaps, after all, I have not
handled well enough to make worth the acknow-

ledgment,—the simile of the patches of moss to
sunshine, in the second canto, was borrowed from
Gilpin's Forest Scenery:—that of unfortunate
poets to crushed perfumes, in the fourth, from
one about good men in adversity in Bacon's
Apophthegms;—Giovanni's praise of his dead
brother, from the panegyric pronounced over
Launcelot of the Lake, which the reader may
find in Ellis's Specimens of Early Romances;—
and part of the description of the nymphs, in the
third canto, from Poussin's exquisite picture of
Polyphemus piping on the mountain.

For the same reason, I suppress a good deal
which I had intended to say on the versification
of the poem,—or of that part of it, at least, where,
in coming upon household matters calculated to
touch us nearest, it takes leave, as it were, of a
more visible march and accompaniment. I do not
hesitate to say however, that Pope and the French

school of versification have known the least on the
subject, of any poets perhaps that ever wrote.
They have mistaken mere smoothness for har-
mony; and, in fact, wrote as they did, because
their ears were only sensible of a marked and
uniform regularity. One of the most successful
of Pope's imitators, Dr. Johnson, was confessedly
insensible to music. In speaking of such men, I
allude, of course, only to their style in poetry, and
not to their undisputed excellence in other mat-
ters. The great masters of modern versification
are, Dryden for common narrative, though he
wanted sentiment, and his style in some respects
was apt to be artificial,—Spenser, who was musi-
cal from pure taste,—Milton, who was learnedly
so,—Ariosto, whose fine ear and animal spirits
gave so frank and exquisite a tone to all he said,
—Shakspeare, whose versification escapes us,
only because he over-informed it with knowledge

and sentiment;—and, though the name may appear singular to those who have not read him with due attention to the nature of the language then existing,—Chaucer,—to whom it sometimes appears to me, that I can trace Dryden himself, though the latter spoke on the subject without much relish, or, in fact, knowledge of it. All these are about as different from Pope, as the church organ is from the bell in the steeple, or, to give him a more decorous comparison, the song of the nightingale, from that of the cuckoo.

With the endeavour to recur to a freer spirit of versification, I have joined one of still greater importance,—that of having a free and idiomatic cast of language. There is a cant of art as well as of nature, though the former is not so unpleasant as the latter, which affects non-affectation. But the proper language of poetry is in fact nothing different from that of real life, and depends for its dignity upon the strength and sentiment of what it speaks. It is only adding musical modulation to what a fine understanding might actually utter in the midst of its griefs or enjoyments. The poet therefore should do as Chaucer or Shakspeare did,—not copy what is obsolete or peculiar in either, any more than they copied from their predecessors,—but use as much as possible an actual, existing language,— omitting of course *mere* vulgarisms and fugitive phrases, which are the cant of ordinary discourse, just as tragedy phrases, dead idioms, and exaggerations of dignity, are of the artificial style, and yeas, verilys, and exaggerations of simplicity, are of the natural. The artificial style, it is true, has its beauties, as some great poets have proved; but I am here speaking of the style that is most beautiful; and those poets, it is to be observed, were not the greatest. Of the style, to which

I allude, exquisite specimens, making allowances
for what is obsolete, are to be found in the Can-
terbury Tales of Chaucer, and his Troilus and
Cressida; and you have only to open the first
books of Pulci and Ariosto to meet with two
charming ones, the interview of Orlando with the
Abbot, in the Morgante Maggiore (canto 1. to-
wards the conclusion), and the flight of Angelica,
her meeting with Rinaldo's horse, &c. in the
Orlando Furioso. Homer abounds with them,
though, by the way, not in the translation;
and I need not, of course, warn any reader of
taste against trusting Mr. Hoole for a proper re-
presentation of the delightful Italian. Such ver-
sions, more or less, resemble bad engravings, in
which all the substances, whether flesh, wood, or
cloth, are made of one texture, and that a bad
one. With the Greek dramatists I am ashamed
to say I am unacquainted; and of the Latin

writers, though Horace, for his delightful com-
panionship, is my favourite, Catullus appears to
me to have the truest taste for nature. But an
Englishman need go no further than Shakspeare.
Take a single speech of Lear's; such for instance
as that heart-rending one,

I am a very foolish foud old man,
Fourscore and upwards, &c.

and you have all that criticism can say, or poetry
can do.

In making these observations, I do not demand
the reader to conclude that I have succeeded in
my object, whatever may be my own opinion of
the matter. All the merit I claim is that of hav-
ing made an attempt to describe natural things in
a language becoming them, and to do something
towards the revival of what appears to me a pro-
per English versification. There are narrative
poets now living who have fine eyes for the truth

of things, and it remains with them perhaps to perfect what I may suggest. If I have succeeded at all, the lovers of nature have still to judge in what proportion the success may be;—but let me take them with me a while, whether in doors or out of doors, whether in the room or the green fields,—let my verses, in short, come under the perusal of ingenuous eyes, and be felt a little by the hearts that look out of them, and I am satisfied.

THE

# STORY OF RIMINI.

---

TIME, THE CLOSE OF THE 13TH CENTURY;—SCENE, FIRST
AT RAVENNA, AFTERWARDS AT RIMINI.

# STORY OF RIMINI.

## CANTO I.

*The coming to fetch the Bride from Ravenna.*

THE sun is up, and 'tis a morn of May
Round old Ravenna's clear-shewn towers and bay,
A morn, the loveliest which the year has seen,
Last of the spring, yet fresh with all its green;
For a warm eve, and gentle rains at night,
Have left a sparkling welcome for the light,
And there's a crystal clearness all about;
The leaves are sharp, the distant hills look out;
A balmy briskness comes upon the breeze;
The smoke goes dancing from the cottage trees;

B 2

And when you listen, you may hear a coil
Of bubbling springs about the grassy soil;
And all the scene, in short—sky, earth, and sea,
Breathes like a bright-eyed face, that laughs out
    openly.

'Tis nature, full of spirits, waked and springing:—
The birds to the delicious time are singing,
Darting with freaks and snatches up and down,
Where the light woods go seaward from the town;
While happy faces, striking through the green
Of leafy roads, at every turn are seen;
And the far ships, lifting their sails of white
Like joyful hands, come up with scattery light,
Come gleaming up, true to the wished-for day,
And chase the whistling brine, and swirl into the bay.

And well may all who can, come crowding there,
If peace returning, and processions rare,

5

And to crown all, a marriage in May weather,
Have aught to bring enjoying hearts together;
For on this sparkling day, Ravenna's pride,
The daughter of their prince, becomes a bride,
A bride, to crown the comfort of the land:
And he, whose victories have obtained her hand,
Has taken with the dawn, so flies report,
His promised journey to the expecting court
With hasting pomp, and squires of high degree,
The bold Giovanni, lord of Rimini.

Already in the streets the stir grows loud
Of expectation and a bustling crowd.
With feet and voice the gathering hum contends,
The deep talk heaves, the ready laugh ascends:
Callings, and clapping doors, and curs unite,
And shouts from mere exuberance of delight,
And armed bands, making important way,
Gallant and grave, the lords of holiday,

And nodding neighbours, greeting as they run,
And pilgrims, chanting in the morning sun.
With heaved-out tapestry the windows glow,
By lovely faces brought, that come and go;
Till, the work smoothed, and all the street attired,
They take their seats, with upward gaze admired;
Some looking down, some forwards or aside,
As suits the conscious charm in which they pride;
Some turning a trim waist, or o'er the flow
Of crimson cloths hanging a hand of snow;
But all with smiles prepared, and garlands green,
And all in fluttering talk, impatient for the scene.

And hark! the approaching trumpets, with a start,
On the smooth wind come dancing to the heart.
A moment's hush succeeds; and from the walls,
Firm and at once, a silver answer calls.
Then heave the crowd; and all, who best can strive
In shuffling struggle, tow'rd the palace drive,

Where balconied and broad, of marble fair,
On pillars it o'erlooks the public square;
For there Duke Guido is to hold his state
With his fair daughter, seated o'er the gate:—
But the full place rejects the invading tide;
And after a rude heave from side to side,
With angry faces turned, and feet regained,
The peaceful press with order is maintained,
Leaving the door-ways only for the crowd,
The space within for the procession proud.

For in this manner is the square set out:—
The sides, path-deep, are crowded round about,
And faced with guards, who keep the road entire;
And opposite to these, a brilliant quire
Of knights and ladies hold the central spot,
Seated in groups upon a grassy plot;
The seats with boughs are shaded from above
Of early trees transplanted from a grove,

And in the midst, fresh whistling through the scene,
A lightsome fountain starts from out the green,
Clear and compact, till, at its height o'er-run,
It shakes its loosening silver in the sun.

There, talking with the ladies, you may see,
Standing about, or seated, frank and free,
Some of the finest warriors of the court,—
Baptist, and Hugo of the princely port,
And Azo, and Obizo, and the grace
Of frank Esmeriald with his open face,
And Felix the Fine Arm, and him who well
Repays his lavish honours, Lionel,
Besides a host of spirits, nursed in glory,
Fit for sweet woman's love and for the poet's story.

There too, in thickest of the bright-eyed throng,
Stands the young father of Italian song,

Guy Cavalcanti, of a knightly race;
The poet looks out in his earnest face;
He with the pheasant's plume—there—bending now,
Something he speaks around him with a bow,
And all the listening looks, with nods and flushes,
Break round him into smiles and sparkling blushes.

Another start of trumpets, with reply;
And o'er the gate a sudden canopy
Raises, on ivory shafts, a crimson shade,
And Guido issues with the princely maid,
And sits;—the courtiers fall on either side;
But every look is fixed upon the bride,
Who pensive comes at first, and hardly hears
The enormous shout that springs as she appears,
Till, as she views the countless gaze below,
And faces that with grateful homage glow,
A home to leave, and husband yet to see,
Fade in the warmth of that great charity;

And hard it is, she thinks, to have no will;
But not to bless these thousands, harder still:
With that, a keen and quivering glance of tears
Scarce moves her patient mouth, and disappears;
A smile is underneath, and breaks away,
And round she looks and breathes, as best befits the
    day.

What need I tell of lovely lips and eyes,
A clipsome waist, and bosom's balmy rise,
The dress of bridal white, and the dark curls
Bedding an airy coronet of pearls?
There's not in all that crowd one gallant being,
Whom if his heart were whole, and rank agreeing,
It would not fire to twice of what he is,
To clasp her to his heart, and call her his.

While thus with tip-toe looks the people gaze,
Another shout the neighb'ring quarters raise:

The train are in the town, and gathering near,
With noise of cavalry, and trumpets clear;
A princely music, unbedinned with drums:
The mighty brass seems opening as it comes,
And now it fills, and now it shakes the air,
And now it bursts into the sounding square;
At which the crowd with such a shout rejoice,
Each thinks he's deafened with his neighbour's voice.
Then, with a long-drawn breath, the clangours die;
The palace trumpets give a last reply,
And clattering hoofs succeed, with stately stir
Of snortings proud and clinking furniture:
It seems as if the harnessed war were near;
But in their garb of peace the train appear,
Their swords alone reserved, but idly hung,
And the chains freed by which their shields were slung.

First come the trumpeters, clad all in white
Except the breast, which wears a scutcheon bright.

By four and four they ride, on horses grey;
And as they sit along their easy way,
Stately, and heaving to the sway below,
Each plants his trumpet on his saddle-bow.

The heralds next appear, in vests attired
Of stiffening gold with radiant colours fired;
And then the pursuivants, who wait on these,
All dressed in painted richness to the knees:
Each rides a dappled horse, and bears a shield,
Charged with three heads upon a golden field.

Twelve ranks of squires come after, twelve in one
With forked pennons lifted in the sun,
Which tell, as they look backward in the wind,
The bearings of the knights that ride behind.
Their steeds are ruddy bay; and every squire
His master's colour shews in his attire.

These past, and at a lordly distance, come
The knights themselves, and fill the quickening hum,
The flower of Rimini.   Apart they ride,
Six in a row, and with a various pride;
But all as fresh as fancy could desire,
All shapes of gallantry on steeds of fire.

Differing in colours is the knights' array,
The horses, black and chesnut, roan and bay;—
The horsemen, crimson vested, purple, and white,—
All but the scarlet cloak for every knight,
Which thrown apart, and hanging loose behind,
Rests on his steed, and ruffles in the wind.
Their caps of velvet have a lightsome fit,
Each with a dancing feather sweeping it,
Tumbling its white against their short dark hair;
But what is of the most accomplished air,
All wear memorials of their lady's love,
A ribbon, or a scarf, or silken glove,

Some tied about their arm, some at the breast,
Some, with a drag, dangling from the cap's crest.

A suitable attire the horses shew;
Their golden bits keep wrangling as they go;
The bridles glance about with gold and gems;
And the rich housing-cloths, above the hems
Which comb along the ground with golden pegs,
Are half of net, to shew the hinder legs.
Some of the cloths themselves are golden thread
With silk enwoven, azure, green, or red;
Some spotted on a ground of different hue,
As burning stars upon a cloth of blue,—
Or purple smearings with a velvet light
Rich from the glary yellow thickening bright,—
Or a spring green, powdered with April posies,—
Or flush vermilion, set with silver roses :
But all are wide and large, and with the wind,
When it comes fresh, go sweeping out behind.

With various earnestness the crowd admire
Horsemen and horse, the motion and the attire.
Some watch, as they go by, the riders' faces
Looking composure, and their knightly graces;
The life, the carelessness, the sudden heed,
The body curving to the rearing steed,
The patting hand, that best persuades the check,
And makes the quarrel up with a proud neck,
The thigh broad pressed, the spanning palm upon it,
And the jerked feather swaling in the bonnet.

Others the horses and their pride explore,
Their jauntiness behind and strength before;
The flowing back, firm chest, and fetlocks clean,
The branching veins ridging the glossy lean,
The mane hung sleekly, the projecting eye
That to the stander near looks awfully,
The finished head, in its compactness free,
Small, and o'rearching to the lifted knee,

The start and snatch, as if they felt the comb,
With mouths that fling about the creamy foam,
The snorting turbulence, the nod, the champing,
The shift, the tossing, and the fiery tramping.

And now the Princess, pale and with fixed eye,
Perceives the last of those precursors nigh,
Each rank uncovering, as they pass in state,
Both to the courtly fountain and the gate.
And then a second interval succeeds
Of stately length, and then a troop of steeds
Milkwhite and unattired, Arabian bred,
Each by a blooming boy lightsomely led:
In every limb is seen their faultless race,
A fire well tempered, and a free left grace:
Slender their spotless shapes, and meet the sight
With freshness, after all those colours bright:
And as with quoit-like drop their steps they bear,
They lend their streaming tails to the fond air.

These for a princely present are divined,
And shew the giver is not far behind.
The talk increases now, and now advance,
Space after space, with many a sprightly prance,
The pages of the court, in rows of three;
Of white and crimson is their livery.
Space after space,—and yet the attendants come,—
And deeper goes about the impatient hum—
Ah—yes—no—'tis not he—but 'tis the squires
Who go before him when his pomp requires;
And now his huntsman shews the lessening train,
Now the squire-carver, and the chamberlain,—
And now his banner comes, and now his shield
Borne by the squire that waits him to the field,—
And then an interval,—a lordly space;—
A pin-drop silence strikes o'er all the place:
The princess, from a distance, scarcely knows
Which way to look; her colour comes and goes;

c

And with an impulse and affection free
She lays her hand upon her father's knee,
Who looks upon her with a laboured smile,
Gathering it up into his own the while,
When some one's voice, as if it knew not how
To check itself, exclaims, "the prince! now—now!"
And on a milk-white courser, like the air,
A glorious figure springs into the square;
Up, with a burst of thunder, goes the shout,
And rolls the trembling walls and peopled roofs
    about.

Never was nobler finish of fine sight;
'Twas like the coming of a shape of light;
And every lovely gazer, with a start,
Felt the quick pleasure smite across her heart:—
The princess, who at first could scarcely see,
Though looking still that way from dignity,

Gathers new courage as the praise goes round,

And bends her eyes to learn what they have found.

And see,—his horse obeys the check unseen;

And with an air 'twixt ardent and serene,

Letting a fall of curls about his brow,

He takes his cap off with a gallant bow;

Then for another and a deafening shout;

And scarfs are waved, and flowers come fluttering

      out;    -

And, shaken by the noise, the reeling air

Sweeps with a giddy whirl among the fair,

And whisks their garments, and their shining hair.


With busy interchange of wonder glows

The crowd, and loves his brilliance as he goes,—

The golden-fretted cap, the downward feather,—

The crimson vest fitting with pearls together,—

The rest in snowy white from the mid thigh :

These catch the extrinsic and the common eye :

But on his shape the gentler sight attends,
Moves as he passes,—as he bends him, bends,—
Watches his air, his gesture, and his face,
And thinks it never saw such manly grace,
So fine are his bare throat, and curls of black,—
So lightsomely dropt in, his lordly back—
His thigh so fitted for the tilt or dance,
So heaped with strength, and turned with elegance;
But above all, so meaning is his look,
Full, and as readable as open book;
And so much easy dignity there lies
In the frank lifting of his cordial eyes.

His haughty steed, who seems by turns to be
Vexed and made proud by that cool mastery,
Shakes at his bit, and rolls his eyes with care,
Reaching with stately step at the fine air;
And now and then, sideling his restless pace,
Drops with his hinder legs, and shifts his place,

And feels through all his frame a fiery thrill:
The princely rider on his back sits still,
And looks where'er he likes, and sways him at his
    will.


Surprise, relief, a joy scarce understood,
Something perhaps of very gratitude,
And fifty feelings, undefin'd and new,
Dance through the bride, and flush her faded hue.
" Could I but once," she thinks; " securely place
A trust for the contents on such a case,
And know the spirit that should fill that dwelling,
This chance of mine would hardly be compelling."
Just then, the stranger, coming slowly round
By the clear fountain and the brilliant ground,
And bending, as he goes, with frequent thanks,
Beckons a follower to him from the ranks,
And loosening, as he speaks, from its light hold
A dropping jewel with its chain of gold,

Sends it, in token he had loved him long,
To the young father of Italian song:
The youth smiles up, and with a lowly grace
Bending his lifted eyes and blushing face,
Looks after his new friend, who, scarcely gone
In the wide turning, nods and passes on,

This is sufficient for the destined bride;
She took an interest first, but now a pride;
And as the prince comes riding to the place,
Baring his head, and raising his fine face,
She meets his full obeisance with an eye
Of self-permission and sweet gravity;
He looks with touched respect, and gazes, and goes
    by.

# CANTO II.

# CANTO II.

---

*The Bride's Journey to Rimini.*

We'll pass the followers, and their closing state;
The court was entered by a hinder gate;
The duke and princess had retired before,
Joined by the knights and ladies at the door;
But something seemed amiss, and there ensued
Deep talk among the spreading multitude,
Who got in clumps, or paced the measured street,
Filling with earnest hum the noontide heat;
Nor ceased the wonder, as the day increased,
And brought no symptoms of a bridal feast,

No mass, no tilt, no largess for the crowd,
Nothing to answer that procession proud;
But a blank look, as if no court had been;
Silence without, and secrecy within;
And nothing heard by listening at the walls,
But now and then a bustling through the halls,
Or the dim organ roused at gathering intervals.

The truth was this :—The bridegroom had not come,
But sent his brother, proxy in his room.
A lofty spirit the former was, and proud,
Little gallant, and had a sort of cloud
Hanging for ever on his cold address,
Which he mistook for proper manliness.
But more of this hereafter.  Guido knew
The prince's character; and he knew too,
That sweet as was his daughter, and prepared
To do her duty, where appeal was barred,

She had stout notions on the marrying score,
And where the match unequal prospect bore,
Might pause with firmness, and refuse to strike.
A chord her own sweet music so unlike.
The old man therefore, kind enough at heart,
Yet fond from habit of intrigue and art,
And little formed for sentiments like these,
Which seemed to him mere maiden niceties,
Had thought at once to gratify the pride
Of his stern neighbour, and secure the bride,
By telling him, that if, as he had heard,
Busy he was just then, 'twas but a word,
And he might send and wed her by another,—
Of course, no less a person than his brother.
The bride meantime was told, and not unmoved,
To look for one no sooner seen than loved;
And when Giovanni, struck with what he thought
Mere proof how his triumphant hand was sought,

Dispatched the wished for prince, who was a creatur
Formed in the very poetry of nature,
The effect was perfect, and the future wife
Caught in the elaborate snare, perhaps for life.

One shock there was, however, to sustain,
Which nigh restored her to herself again.
She saw, when all were housed, in Guido's face
A look of leisurely surprise take place;
A little whispering followed for a while,
And then 'twas told her with an easy smile,
That Prince Giovanni, to his great chagrin,
Had been delayed by something unforeseen,
But rather than defer his day of bliss
(If his fair ruler took it not amiss)
Had sent his brother Paulo in his stead;
" Who," said old Guido, with a nodding head,
" May well be said to represent his brother,
For when you see the one, you know the other."

By this time Paulo joined them where they stood,

And, seeing her in some uneasy mood,

Changed the mere cold respects his brother sent

To such a strain of cordial compliment,

And paid them with an air so frank and bright,

As to a friend appreciated at sight,

That air, in short, which sets you at your ease,

Without implying your perplexities,

That what with the surprise in every way,

The hurry of the time, the appointed day,

The very shame which now appeared increased,

Of begging leave to have her hand released,

And above all, those tones, and smiles, and looks,

Which seemed to realize the dreams of books,

And helped her genial fancy to conclude

That fruit of such a stock must all be good,

She knew not how to object in her confusion;

Quick were the marriage-rites; and, in conclusion,

The proxy, turning midst the general hush,
Kissed her meek lips, betwixt a rosy blush.


At last, about the vesper hour, a score
Of trumpets issued from the palace door,
The banners of their brass with favours tied,
And with a blast proclaimed the wedded bride.
But not a word the sullen silence broke,
Till something of a gift the herald spoke,
And with a bag of money issuing out,
Scattered the ready harvest round about;
Then burst the mob into a jovial cry,
And largess! largess! claps against the sky,
And bold Giovanni's name, the lord of Rimini.


The rest however still were looking on,
Careless and mute, and scarce the noise was gone,
When riding from the gate, with banners reared,
Again the morning visitors appeared.

## 31.

The prince was in his place; and in a car,
Before him, glistening like a farewell star,
Sate the dear lady with her brimming eyes;
And off they set, through doubtful looks and cries;
For some too shrewdly guessed, and some were vexed
At the dull day, and some the whole perplexed;
And all great pity thought it to divide
Two that seemed made for bridegroom and for bride.
Ev'n she, whose heart this strange, abrupt event
Had seared, as 'twere, with burning wonderment,
Could scarce, at times, a passionate cry forbear
At leaving her own home and native air;
Till passing now the limits of the town,
And on the last few gazers looking down,
She saw by the road-side an aged throng,
Who wanting power to bustle with the strong,
Had learnt their gracious mistress was to go,
And gathered there, an unconcerted shew;

Bending they stood, with their old foreheads bare,
And the winds fingered with their reverend hair.
Farewell! farewell, my friends! she would have cried,
But in her throat the leaping accents died,
And, waving with her hand a vain adieu,
She dropt her veil, and backwarder withdrew,
And let the kindly tears their own good course pursue.

It was a lovely evening, fit to close
A lovely day, and brilliant in repose.
Warm, but not dim, a glow was in the air;
The softened breeze came smoothing here and there;
And every tree, in passing, one by one,
Gleamed out with twinkles of the golden sun:
For leafy was the road, with tall array,
On either side, of mulberry and bay,
And distant snatches of blue hills between;
And there the alder was with its bright green,

And the broad chesnut, and the poplar's shoot,
That like a feather waves from head to foot,
With, ever and anon, majestic pines;
And still from tree to tree the early vines
Hung garlanding the way in amber lines.

Nor long the princess kept her from the view
Of that dear scenery with its parting hue:
For sitting now, calm from the gush of tears,
With dreaming eye fixed down, and half-shut ears,
Hearing, yet hearing not, the fervent sound
Of hoofs thick reckoning and the wheel's moist round,
A call of " slower!" from the farther part
Of the checked riders, woke her with a start;
And looking up again, half sigh, half stare,
She lifts her veil, and feels the freshening air.

'Tis down a hill they go, gentle indeed,
And such, as with a bold and pranksome speed

D

Another time they would have scorned to measure;
But now they take with them a lovely treasure,
And feel they should consult her gentle pleasure.


And now with thicker shades the pines appear;
The noise of hoofs grows duller to her ear ;
And quitting suddenly their gravelly toil,
The wheels go spinning o'er a sandy soil.
Here first the silence of the country seems
To come about her with its listening dreams,
And, full of anxious thoughts, half freed from pain,
In downward musing she relapsed again,
Leaving the others who had passed that way
In careless spirits of the early day,
To look about, and mark the reverend scene,
For awful tales renowned, and everlasting green.


A heavy spot the forest looks at first,
To one grim shade condemnèd, and sandy thirst,

Or only chequered, here and there, with bushes
Dusty and sharp, or plashy pools with rushes,
About whose sides the swarming insects fry,
Opening with noisome din, as they go by.
But entering more and more, they quit the sand
At once, and strike upon a grassy land,
From which the trees, as from a carpet, rise
In knolls and clumps, with rich varieties.
A moment's trouble find the knights to rein
Their horses in, which, feeling turf again,
Thrill, and curvet, and long to be at large
To scour the space and give the winds a charge,
Or pulling tight the bridles, as they pass,
Dip their warm mouths into the freshening grass.
But soon in easy rank, from glade to glade,
Proceed they, coasting underneath the shade,
Some baring to the cool their placid brows,
Some looking upward through the glimmering
    boughs,

Or peering grave through inward-opening places,
And half prepared for glimpse of shadowy faces.
Various the trees and passing foliage here,—
Wild pear, and oak, and dusky juniper,
With briony between in trails of white,
And ivy, and the suckle's streaky light,
And moss, warm gleaming with a sudden mark,
Like flings of sunshine left upon the bark,
And still the pine, long-haired, and dark, and tall,
In lordly right, predominant o'er all.

Much they admire that old religious tree
With shaft above the rest up-shooting free,
And shaking, when its dark locks feel the wind,
Its wealthy fruit with rough Mosaic rind.
At noisy intervals, the living cloud
Of cawing rooks breaks o'er them, gathering loud
Like a wild people at a stranger's coming;
Then hushing paths succeed, with insects humming,

Or ring-dove, that repeats his pensive plea,
Or startled gull, up-screaming tow'rds the sea.
But scarce their eyes encounter living thing,
Save, now and then, a goat loose wandering,
Or a few cattle, looking up aslant
With sleepy eyes and meek mouths ruminant;
Or once, a plodding woodman, old and bent,
Passing with half-indifferent wonderment,
Yet turning, at the last, to look once more;
Then feels his trembling staff, and onward as before.

So ride they pleased,—till now the couching sun
Levels his final look through shadows dun;
And the clear moon, with meek o'er-lifted face,
Seems come to look into the silvering place.
Then first the bride waked up, for then was heard,
Sole voice, the poet's and the lover's bird,
Preluding first, as if the sounds were cast
For the dear leaves about her, till at last

With shot-out raptures, in a perfect shower,
She vents her heart on the delicious hour.
Lightly the horsemen go, as if they'd ride
A velvet path, and hear no voice beside:
A placid hope assures the breath-suspended bride.

So ride they in delight through beam and shade;–
Till many a rill now passed, and many a glade,
They quit the piny labyrinths, and soon
Emerge into the full and sheeted moon:
Chilling it seems; and pushing steed on steed,
They start them freshly with a homeward speed.
Then well-known fields they pass, and stragglir
    cots,
Boy-storied trees, and passion-plighted spots;
And turning last a sudden corner, see
The square-lit towers of slumbering Rimini.
The marble bridge comes heaving forth below
With a long gleam; and nearer as they go,

They see the still Marecchia, cold and bright,

Sleeping along with face against the light.

A hollow trample now,—a fall of chains,—

The bride has entered,—not a voice remains;—

Night, and a maiden silence, wrap the plains.

# CANTO III.

# CANTO III.

———

*The Fatal Passion.*

Now why must I disturb a dream of bliss,
Or bring cold sorrow 'twixt the wedded kiss?
Sad is the strain, with which I cheer my long
And caged hours, and try my native tongue*;
Now too, while rains autumnal, as I sing,
Wash the dull bars, chilling my sicklied wing,
And all the climate presses on my sense;
But thoughts it furnishes of things far hence,

* The preceding canto, and a small part of the present, were
written in prison.

And leafy dreams affords me, and a feeling
Which I should else disdain, tear-dipped and healing;
And shews me,—more than what it first designed,—
How little upon earth our home we find,
Or close the intended course of erring human-kind.

Enough of this.  Yet how shall I disclose
The weeping days that with the morning rose,
How bring the bitter disappointment in,—
The holy cheat, the virtue-binding sin,—
The shock, that told this lovely, trusting heart,
That she had given, beyond all power to part,
Her hope, belief, love, passion, to one brother,
Possession (oh, the misery!) to another!

Some likeness was there 'twixt the two,—an air
At times, a cheek, a colour of the hair,
A tone, when speaking of indifferent things;
Nor, by the scale of common measurings,

Would you say more perhaps, than that the one
Was more robust, the other finelier spun;
That of the two, Giovanni was the graver,
Paulo the livelier, and the more in favour.

Some tastes there were indeed, that would prefer
Giovanni's countenance as the martialler;
And 'twas a soldier's truly, if an eye
Ardent and cool at once, drawn-back and high,
An eagle's nose, and a determined lip,
Were the best marks of manly soldiership.
Paulo's was fashioned in a different mould,
And finer still, I think; for though 'twas bold,
When boldness was required, and could put on
A glowing frown, as if an angel shone,
Yet there was nothing in it one might call
A stamp exclusive, or professional,—
No courtier's face, and yet its smile was ready,—
No scholar's, yet its look was deep and steady,—

No soldier's, for its power was all of mind,
Too true for violence, and too refined.
A graceful nose was his, lightsomely brought
Down from a forehead of clear-spirited thought;
Wisdom looked sweet and inward from his eye;
And round his mouth was sensibility:—
It was a face, in short, seemed made to shew
How far the genuine flesh and blood could go;—
A morning glass of unaffected nature,
Something, that baffled every pompous feature,—
The visage of a glorious human creature.

If any points there were, at which they came
Nearer together, 'twas in knightly fame,
And all accomplishments that art may know,—
Hunting, and princely hawking, and the bow,
The rush together in the bright-eyed list,
Fore-thoughted chess, the riddle rarely missed,

And the decision of still knottier points,
With knife in hand, of boar and peacock joints,—
Things, that·might shake the fame that Tristan got,
And bring a doubt on perfect Launcelot.
But leave we knighthood to the former part;
The tale I tell is of the human heart.

The worst of Prince Giovanni, as his bride
Too quickly found, was an ill-tempered pride.
Bold, handsome, able if he chose to please,
Punctual and ·right in common offices,
He lost the sight of conduct's only worth,
The scattering smiles on this uneasy earth,
And·on the strength of virtues of small weight,
Claimed tow'rds himself the exercise of great.
He kept no reckoning with his sweets and sours;—
He'd hold a· sullen countenance for hours,
And then, if pleased to cheer himself a space,
Look for the immediate rapture in your face,

And wonder that a cloud could still be there,
How small soever, when his own was fair.
Yet such is conscience,—so designed to keep
Stern, central watch, though all things else go
    sleep,
And so much knowledge of one's self there lies
Cored, after all, in our complacencies,
That no suspicion would have touched him more,
Than that of wanting on the generous score:
He would have whelmed you with a weight of scorn,
Been proud at eve, inflexible at morn,
In short, ill-tempered for a week to come,
And all to strike that desperate error dumb.
Taste had he, in a word, for high-turned merit,
But not the patience, or the genial spirit;
And so he made, 'twixt virtue and defect,
A sort of fierce demand on your respect,
Which, if assisted by his high degree,
It gave him in some eyes a dignity,

And struck a meaner deference in the many,
Left him, at last, unloveable with any.


From this complexion in the reigning brother,
His younger birth perhaps had saved the other.
Born to a homage less gratuitous,
He learned to win a nobler for his house;
And both from habit and a genial heart,
Without much trouble of the reasoning art,
Found this the wisdom and the sovereign good,—
To be, and make, as happy as he could.
Not that he saw, or thought he saw, beyond
His general age, and could not be as fond
Of wars and creeds as any of his race,—
But most he loved a happy human face;
And wheresoe'er his fine, frank eyes were thrown,
He struck the looks he wished for with his own.
*His* danger was, lest, feeling as he did,
Too lightly he might leap o'er means forbid,

And in some tempting hour lose sight of crime
O'er some sweet face too happy for the time;
But fears like these he never entertained,
And had they crossed him, would have been dis
    dained.
Warm was his youth, 'tis true,—nor had been free
From lighter loves,—but virtue reverenced he,
And had been kept from men of pleasure's cares
By dint of feelings still more warm than theirs.
So what but service leaped where'er he went!
Was there a tilt-day or a tournament,—
For welcome grace there rode not such another,
Nor yet for strength, except his lordly brother.
Was there a court-day, or a sparkling feast,
Or better still,—in my ideas, at least,—
A summer party to the greenwood shade,
With lutes prepared, and cloth on herbage laid,
And ladies' laughter coming through the air,—
He was the readiest and the blithest there;

And made the time so exquisitely pass
With stories told with elbow on the grass,
Or touched the music in his turn so finely,
That all he did, they thought, was done divinely.

The lovely stranger could not fail to see
Too soon this difference, more especially
As her consent, too lightly now, she thought,
With hopes far different had been strangely bought;
And many a time the pain of that neglect
Would strike in blushes o'er her self-respect:
But since the ill was cureless, she applied
With busy virtue to resume her pride,
And hoped to value her submissive heart
On playing well a patriot daughter's part,
Trying her new-found duties to prefer
To what a father might have owed to her.
The very day too when her first surprise
Was full, kind tears had come into her eyes

On finding, by his care, her private room
Furnished, like magic, from her own at home;
The very books and all transported there,
The leafy tapestry, and the crimson chair,
The lute, the glass that told the shedding hours,
The little urn of silver for the flowers,
The frame for broidering, with a piece half done,
And the white falcon, basking in the sun,
Who, when he saw her, sidled on his stand,
And twined his neck against her trembling hand.
But what had touched her nearest, was the thought,
That if 'twere destined for her to be brought
To a sweet mother's bed, the joy would be
Giovanni's too, and his her family:—
He seemed already father of her child,
And on the nestling pledge in patient thought she
    smiled.
Yet then a pang would cross her, and the red
In either downward cheek startle and spread,

To think that he, who was to have such part
In joys like these, had never shared her heart;
But back she chased it with a sigh austere;
And did she chance, at times like these, to hear
Her husband's footstep, she would haste the more,
And with a double smile open the door,
And ask him after all his morning's doing,
How his new soldiers pleased him in reviewing,
Or if the boar was slain, which he had been pursuing.

The prince, at this, would bend on her an eye
Cordial enough, and kiss her tenderly;
Nor, to say truly, was he slow in common
To accept the attentions of this lovely woman;
But then meantime he took no generous pains,
By mutual pleasing, to secure his gains;
He entered not, in turn, in her delights,
Her books, her flowers, her taste for rural sights;

Nay, scarcely her sweet singing minded he,
Unless his pride was roused by company;
Or when to please him, after martial play,
She strained her lute to some old fiery lay
Of fierce Orlando, or of Ferumbras,
Or Ryan's cloak, or how by the red grass
In battle you might know where Richard was.

Yet all the while, no doubt, however stern
Or cold at times, he thought he loved in turn,
And that the joy he took in her sweet ways,
The pride he felt when she excited praise,
In short, the enjoyment of his own good pleasure,
Was thanks enough, and passion beyond measure.

She, had she loved him, might have thought so too:
For what will love's exalting not go through,
Till long neglect, and utter selfishness,
Shame the fond pride it takes in its distress?

But ill prepared was she, in her hard lot,
To fancy merit where she found it not,—
She, who had been beguiled,—she, who was made.
Within a gentle bosom to be laid,—
To bless and to be blessed,—to be heart-bare
To one who found his bettered likeness there,—
To think for ever with him, like a bride,—
To haunt his eye, like taste personified,—
To double his delight, to share his sorrow,
And like a morning beam, wake to him every morrow.

Paulo, meantime, who ever since the day
He saw her sweet looks bending o'er his way,
Had stored them up, unconsciously, as graces
By which to judge all other forms and faces,
Had learnt, I know not how, the secret snare,
Which gave her up, that evening, to his care.
Some babbler, may-be, of old Guido's court,
Or foolish friend had told him, half in sport:

But to his heart the fatal flattery went;
And grave he grew, and inwardly intent,.
And ran back, in his mind, with sudden spring,
Look, gesture, smile, speech, silence, every thing;
Even what before had seemed indifference,
And read them over in another sense.
Then would he blush with sudden self-disdain,
To think how fanciful he was, and vain;
And with half angry, half regretful sigh,
Tossing his chin, and feigning a free eye,
Breathe off, as 'twere, the idle tale, and look
About him for his falcon or his book,
Scorning that ever he should entertain
One thought that in the end might give his broth
    pain.

This start however came so often round,—
So often fell he in deep thought, and found

Occasion to renew his carelessness,

Yet every time the power grown less and less,

That by degrees, half wearied, half inclined,

To the sweet struggling image he resigned ;

And merely, as he thought, to make the best

Of what by force would come about his breast,

Began to bend down his admiring eyes

On all her touching looks and qualities,

Turning their shapely sweetness every way,

Till 'twas his food and habit day by day,

And she became companion of his thought;

Silence her gentleness before him brought,

Society her sense, reading her books,

Music her voice, every sweet thing her looks,

Which sometimes seemed, when he sat fixed awhile,

To steal beneath his eyes with upward smile:

And did he stroll into some lonely place,

Under the trees, upon the thick soft grass,

How charming, would he think, to see her here!
How heightened then, and perfect would appear
The two divinest things this world has got,
A lovely woman in a rural spot!

Thus daily went he on, gathering sweet pain
About his fancy, till it thrilled again;
And if his brother's image, less and less,
Startled him up from his new idleness,
'Twas not,—he fancied,—that he reasoned worse,
Or felt less scorn of wrong, but the reverse.
That one should think of injuring another,
Or trenching on his peace,—this too a brother,—
And all from selfishness and pure weak will,
To him seemed marvellous and impossible.
'Tis true, thought he, one being more there was,
Who might meantime have weary hours to pass,—
One weaker too to bear them,—and for whom?—
No matter;—he could not reverse her doom;

And so he sighed and smiled, as if one thought
Of paltering could suppose that *he* was to be caught.

Yet if she loved him, common gratitude,
If not, a sense of what was fair and good,
Besides his new relationship and right,
Would make him wish to please her all he might;
And as to thinking,—where could be the harm,
If to his heart he kept its secret charm?
He wished not to himself another's blessing,
But then he might console for not possessing;
And glorious things there were, which but to see
And not admire, was mere stupidity:
He might as well object to his own eyes
For loving to behold the fields and skies,
His neighbour's grove, or story-painted hall;
'Twas but the taste for what was natural;
Only his fav'rite thought was loveliest of them all.

Concluding thus, and happier that he knew
His ground so well, near and more near he drew;
And, sanctioned by his brother's manner, spent
Hours by her side as happy as well-meant.
He read with her, he rode, he went a hawking,
He spent still evenings in delightful talking,
While she sat busy at her broidery frame;
Or touched the lute with her, and when they came
To some fine part, prepared her for the pleasure,
And then with double smile stole on the measure.

Then at the tournament,—who there but she
Made him more gallant still than formerly,
Couch o'er his tightened lance with double force,
Pass like the wind, sweeping down man and horse,
And franklier then than ever, midst the shout
And dancing trumpets ride, uncovered, round about?
His brother only, more than hitherto,
He would avoid, or sooner let subdue,

Partly from something strange unfelt before,
Partly because Giovanni sometimes wore
A knot his bride had worked him, green and gold;—
For in all things with nature did she hold;
And while 'twas being worked, her fancy was
Of sunbeams mingling with a tuft of grass.

Francesca from herself but ill could hide
What pleasure now was added to her side,—
How placidly, yet fast, the days succeeded
With one who thought and felt so much as she did,—
And how the chair he sat in, and the room,
Began to look, when he had failed to come.
But as she better knew the cause than he,
She seemed to have the more necessity
For struggling hard, and rousing all her pride;
And so she did at first; she even tried
To feel a sort of anger at his care;
But these extremes brought but a kind despair;

And then she only spoke more sweetly to him,
And found her failing eyes give looks that melted
    through him.

Giovanni too, who felt relieved indeed
To see another to his place succeed,
Or rather filling up some trifling hours,
Better spent elsewhere, and beneath his powers,
Left the new tie to strengthen day by day,
Talked less and less, and longer kept away,
Secure in his self-love and sense of right,
That he was welcome most, come when he might.
And doubtless, they, in their still finer sense,
With added care repaid this confidence,
Turning their thoughts from his abuse of it,
To what on their own parts was graceful and was fit

Ah now, ye gentle pair,—now think awhile,
Now, while ye still can think, and still can smile;

Now, while your generous hearts have not been
    grieved
Perhaps with something not to be retrieved,
And ye have still, within, the power of gladness,
From self-resentment free, and retrospective mad-
    ness!

So did they think;—but partly from delay,
Partly from fancied ignorance of the way,
And most from feeling the bare contemplation
Give them fresh need of mutual consolation,
They scarcely tried to see each other less,
And did but meet with deeper tenderness,
Living, from day to day, as they were used,
Only with graver thoughts, and smiles reduced,
And sighs more frequent, which, when one would
    heave,
The other longed to start up and receive.

For whether some suspicion now had crossed
Giovanni's mind, or whether he had lost
More of his temper lately, he would treat
His wife with petty scorns, and starts of heat,
And, to his own omissions proudly blind,
O'erlook the pains she took to make him kind,
And yet be angry, if he thought them less;
He found reproaches in her meek distress,
Forcing her silent tears, and then resenting,
Then almost angrier grown from half repenting,
And, hinting at the last, that some there were
Better perhaps than he, and tastefuller,
And these, for what he knew,—he little cared,—
Might please her, and be pleased, though he despaired.
Then would he quit the room, and half disdain
Himself for being in so harsh a strain,
And venting thus his temper on a woman;
Yet not the more for that changed he in common,

r took more pains to please her, and be near:—
7hat! should he truckle to a woman's tear?

t times like these the princess tried to shun
he face of Paulo as too kind a one;
nd shutting up her tears with resolute sigh,
'ould walk into the air, and see the sky,
ad feel about her all the garden green,
ad hear the birds that shot the covert boughs
    between.

noble range it was, of many a rood,
'alled round with trees, and ending in a wood:
ideed the whole was leafy; and it had
 winding stream about, clear and glad,
hat danced from shade to shade, and on its way
>emed smiling with delight to feel the day.
here was the pouting rose, both red and white,
he flamy heart's-ease, flushed with purple light,

Blush-hiding strawberry, sunny-coloured box,
Hyacinth, handsome with his clustering locks,
The lady lily, looking gently down,
Pure lavender, to lay in bridal gown,
The daisy, lovely on both sides,—in short,
All the sweet cups to which the bees resort,
With plots of grass, and perfumed walks between
Of citron, honeysuckle and jessamine,
With orange, whose warm leaves so finely suit,
And look as if they'd shade a golden fruit ;
And midst the flowers, turfed round beneath a shade
Of circling pines, a babbling fountain played,
And 'twixt their shafts you saw the water bright,
Which through the darksome tops glimmered with
  showering light.
So now you walked beside an odorous bed
Of gorgeous hues, white, azure, golden, red ;
And now turned off into a leafy walk,
Close and continuous, fit for lovers' talk ;

And now pursued the stream, and as you trod
Onward and onward o'er the velvet sod,
Felt on your face an air, watery and sweet,
And a new sense in your soft-lighting feet;
And then perhaps you entered upon shades,
Pillowed with dells and uplands 'twixt the glades,
Through which the distant palace, now and then,
Looked lordly forth with many-windowed ken;
A land of trees, which reaching round about,
In shady blessing stretched their old arms out,
With spots of sunny opening, and with nooks,
To lie and read in, sloping into brooks,
Where at her drink you started the slim deer,
Retreating lightly with a lovely fear.
And all about, the birds kept leafy house,
And sung and sparkled in and out the boughs;
And all about, a lovely sky of blue
Clearly was felt, or down the leaves laughed through;

And here and there, in every part, were seats,
Some in the open walks, some in retreats;
With bowering leaves o'erhead, to which the eye.
Looked up half sweetly and half awfully,—
Places of nestling green, for poets made,
Where when the sunshine struck a yellow shade,
The slender trunks, to inward peeping sight,
Thronged in dark pillars up the gold green light.

But 'twixt the wood and flowery walks, halfway,
And formed of both, the loveliest portion lay,
A spot, that struck you like enchanted ground :—
It was a shallow dell, set in a mound
Of sloping shrubs, that mounted by degrees,
The birch and poplar mixed with heavier trees;
From under which, sent through a marble spout,
Betwixt the dark wet green, a rill gushed out,
Whose low sweet talking seemed as if it said
Something eternal to that happy shade:

The ground within was lawn, with plots of flowers
Heaped towards the centre, and with citron bowers;
And in the midst of all, clustered about
With bay and myrtle, and just gleaming out,
Lurked a pavilion,—a delicious sight,
Small, marble, well-proportioned, mellowy white,
With yellow vine-leaves sprinkled,—but no more,—
And a young orange either side the door.
The door was to the wood, forward, and square,
The rest was domed at top, and circular;
And through the dome the only light came in,
Tinged, as it entered, with the vine-leaves thin.

It was a beauteous piece of ancient skill,
Spared from the rage of war, and perfect still;
By most supposed the work of fairy hands,
Famed for luxurious taste, and choice of lands,—
Alcina, or Morgana,—who from fights
And errant fame inveigled amorous knights,

And lived with them in a long round of blisses,

Feasts, concerts, baths, and bower-enshaded kisses.

But 'twas a temple, as its sculpture told,

Built to the Nymphs that haunted there of old;

For o'er the door was carved a sacrifice

By girls and shepherds brought, with reverend eyes,

Of sylvan drinks and foods, simple and sweet,

And goats with struggling horns and planted feet:

And on a line with this ran round about

A like relief, touched exquisitely out,

That shewed, in various scenes, the nymphs them-
selves;

Some by the water side on bowery shelves

Leaning at will,—some in the water sporting

With sides half swelling forth, and looks of courting,—

Some in a flowery dell, hearing a swain

. Play on his pipe, till the hills ring again,—

Some tying up their long moist hair,—some sleeping

Under the trees, with fauns and satyrs peeping,—

Or, sidelong-eyed, pretending not to see
The latter in the brakes come creepingly,
While their 'forgotten urns, lying about
In the green herbage, let the water out.
Never, be sure, before or since was seen
A summer-house so fine in such a nest of green.

All the green garden, flower-bed, shade, and plot,
Francesca loved, but most of all this spot.
Whenever she walked forth, wherever went
About the grounds, to this at last she bent:
Here she had brought a lute and a few books;
Here would she lie for hours, with grateful looks,
Thanking at heart the sunshine and the leaves,
The summer rain-drops counting from the eaves,
And all that promising, calm smile we see
In nature's face, when we look patiently.
Then would she think of heaven; and you might hear
Sometimes, when every thing was hushed and clear,

Her gentle voice from out those shades emerging,
Singing the evening anthem to the Virgin.
The gardeners and the rest, who served the place,
And blest whenever they beheld her face,
Knelt when they heard it, bowing and uncovered,
And felt as if in air some sainted beauty hovered.

One day,—'twas on a summer afternoon,
When airs and gurgling brooks are best in tune,
And grasshoppers are loud, and day-work done,
And shades have heavy outlines in the sun,—
The princess came to her accustomed bower
To get her, if she could, a soothing hour,
Trying, as she was used, to leave her cares
Without, and slumberously enjoy the airs,
And the low-talking leaves, and that cool light
The vines let in, and all that hushing sight

Of closing wood seen through the opening door,
And distant plash of waters tumbling o'er,
And smell of citron blooms, and fifty luxuries more.

She tried, as usual, for the trial's sake,
For even that diminished her heart-ache;
And never yet, how ill soe'er at ease,
Came she for nothing 'midst the flowers and trees.
Yet somehow or another, on that day,
She seemed to feel too lightly borne away,—
Too much relieved,—too much inclined to draw
A careless joy from every thing she saw,
And looking round her with a new-born eye,
As if some tree of knowledge had been nigh,
To taste of nature, primitive and free,
And bask at ease in her heart's liberty.

Painfully clear those rising thoughts appeared,
With something dark at bottom that she feared;

And snatching from the fields her thoughtful look,
She reached o'er-head, and took her down a book,
And fell to reading with as fixed an air,
As though she had been wrapt since morning there.

'Twas Launcelot of the Lake, a bright romance,
That like a trumpet, made young pulses dance,
Yet had a softer note that shook still more ;—
She had begun it but the day before,
And read with a full heart, half sweet, half sad,
How old King Ban was spoiled of all he had
But one fair castle : how one summer's day
With his fair queen and child he went away
To ask the great King Arthur for assistance ;
How reaching by himself a hill at distance
He turned to give his castle a last look,
And saw its far white face : and how a smoke,
As he was looking, burst in volumes forth,
And good King Ban saw all that he was worth,

And his fair castle, burning to the ground,
So that his wearied pulse felt over-wound,
And he lay down, and said a prayer apart
For those he loved, and broke his poor old heart.
Then read she of the queen with her young child,
How she came up, and nearly had gone wild,
And how in journeying on in her despair,
She reached a lake and met a lady there,
Who pitied her, and took the baby sweet
Into her arms, when lo, with closing feet
She sprang up all at once, like bird from brake,
And vanished with him underneath the lake.
The mother's feelings we as well may pass :—
The fairy of the place that lady was,
And Launcelot (so the boy was called) became
Her inmate, till in search of knightly fame
He went to Arthur's court, and played his part
So rarely, and displayed so frank a heart,

That what with all his charms of look and limb,
The Queen Geneura fell in love with him:—
And here, with growing interest in her reading,
The princess, doubly fixed, was now proceeding.

Ready she sat with one hand to turn o'er
The leaf, to which her thoughts ran on before,
The other propping her white brow, and throwing
Its ringlets out, under the skylight glowing.
So sat she fixed; and so observed was she
Of one, who at the door stood tenderly,—
Paulo,—who from a window seeing her
Go straight across the lawn, and guessing where,
Had thought she was in tears, and found, that day,
His usual efforts vain to keep away.
" May I come in?" said he:—it made her start,—
That smiling voice;—she coloured, pressed her heart
A moment, as for breath, and then with free
And usual tone said, " O yes,—certainly."

There's apt to be, at conscious times  like these,
An affectation of a bright-eyed ease,
An air of something quite serene and sure,
As if to seem so, was to be, secure :
With this the lovers met, with this they spoke,
With this they sat down to the self-same book,
And Paulo, by degrees, gently embraced
With one permitted arm her lovely waist;
And both their cheeks, like peaches on a tree,
Leaned with a touch together, thrillingly;
And o'er the book they hung, and nothing said,
And every lingering page grew longer as they read.

As thus they sat, and felt with leaps of heart
Their colour change, they came upon the part
Where fond Geneura, with her flame long nurst,
Smiled upon Launcelot when he kissed her first :—
That touch, at last, through every fibre slid;
And Paulo turned, scarce knowing what he did,

Only he felt he could no more dissemble,
And kissed her, mouth to mouth, all in a tremble.
Sad were those hearts, and sweet was that long kiss:
Sacred be love from sight, whate'er it is.
The world was all forgot, the struggle o'er,
Desperate the joy.—That day they read no more.

CANTO·IV.

# CANTO IV.

---

*How the Bride returned to Ravenna.*

It has surprised me often, as I write,
That I, who have of late known small delight,
Should thus pursue a mournful theme, and make
My very solace of distress partake.
And I have longed sometimes, I must confess,
To start at once from notes of wretchedness,
And in a key would make you rise and dance,
Strike up a blithe defiance to mischance.

G

But work begun, an interest in it, shame
At turning coward to the thoughts I frame,
Necessity to keep firm face on sorrow,
Some flattering, sweet-lipped question every morro
And above all, the poet's task divine
Of making tears themselves look up and shine,
And turning to a charm the sorrow past,
Have held me on, and shall do to the last.


Sorrow, to him who has a true touched ear,
Is but the discord of a warbling sphere,
A lurking contrast, which though harsh it be,
Distils the next note more deliciously.
E'en tales like this, founded on real woe,
From bitter seed to balmy fruitage grow:
The woe was earthly, fugitive, is past;
The song that sweetens it, may always last.
And even they, whose shattered hearts and frame
Make them unhappiest of poetic names,

What are they, if they know their calling high,
But crushed perfumes, exhaling to the sky?
Or weeping clouds, that but a while are seen,
Yet keep the earth they haste to, bright and green?

Once, and but once,—nor with a scornful face
Tried worth will hear,—that scene again took place.
Partly by chance they met, partly to see
The spot where they had last gone smilingly,
But most, from failure of all self-support;—
And oh! the meeting in that loved resort!
No peevishness there was, no loud distress,
No mean, recriminating selfishness;
But a mute gush of hiding tears from one
Clasped to the core of him, who yet shed none,—
And self-accusings then, which he began,
And into which her tearful sweetness ran;
And then kind looks, with meeting eyes again,
Starting to deprecate the other's pain;

Till half persuasions they could scarce do wrong,
And sudden sense of wretchedness, more strong,
And—why should I add more?—again they parted,
He doubly torn for her, and she nigh broken-hearted.

She never ventured in that spot again ;
And Paulo knew it, but could not refrain ;
He went again one day; and how it looked!
The calm, old shade !—his presence felt rebuked.
It seemed, as if the hopes of his young heart,
His kindness, and his generous scorn of art,
Had all been a mere dream, or at the best
A vain negation, that could stand no test ;
And that on waking from his idle fit,
He found himself (how could he think of it !)
A selfish boaster, and a hypocrite.

That thought before had grieved him ; but the pain
Cut sharp and sudden, now it came again.

Sick thoughts of late had made his body sick,
And this, in turn, to them grown strangely quick ;
And pale he stood, and seemed to burst all o'er
Into moist anguish never felt before,
And with a dreadful certainty to know,
His peace was gone, and all to come was woe.
Francesca too,—the being, made to bless,—
Destined by him to the same wretchedness,—
It seemed as if such whelming thoughts must find
Some props for them, or he should lose his mind.—
And find he did, not what the worse disease
Of want of charity calls sophistries,—
Nor what can cure a generous heart of pain,—
But humble guesses, helping to sustain.
He thought, with quick philosophy, of things
Rarely found out except through sufferings,—
Of habit, circumstance, design, degree,
Merit, and will, and thoughtful charity :

And these, although they pushed down, as they rose,

His self-respect, and all those morning shews

Of true and perfect, which his youth had built,

Pushed with them too the worst of others guilt;

And furnished him, at least, with something kind,

On which to lean a sad and startled mind:

Till youth, and natural vigour, and the dread

Of self-betrayal, and a thought that spread

From time to time in gladness o'er his face,

That she he loved could have done nothing base,

Helped to restore him to his usual life,

Though grave at heart and with himself at strife;

And he would rise betimes, day after day,

And mount his favourite horse, and ride away

Miles in the country, looking round about,

As he glode by, to force his thoughts without;

And, when he found it vain, would pierce the shade

Of some enwooded field or closer glade,

And there dismounting, idly sit, and sigh,
Or pluck the grass beside him with vague eye,.
And almost envy the poor beast, that went
Cropping it, here and there, with dumb content.
But thus, at least, he exercised his blood,
And kept it livelier than inaction could;
And thus he earned for his thought-working head
The power of sleeping when he went to bed,
And was enabled still to wear away
That task of loaded hearts, another day.

But she, the gentler frame,—the shaken flower,
Plucked up to wither in a foreign bower,—
The struggling, virtue-loving, fallen she,
The wife that was, the mother that might be,—
What could she do, unable thus to keep
Her strength alive, but sit, and think, and weep,
For ever stooping o'er her broidery frame,
Half blind, and longing till the night-time came,

When worn and wearied out with the day's sorrow,
She might be still and senseless till the morrow.

And oh, the morrow, how it used to rise!
How would she open her despairing eyes,
And from the sense of the long lingering day,
Rushing upon her, almost turn away,
Loathing the light, and groan to sleep again!
Then sighing once for all, to meet the pain,
She would get up in haste, and try to pass
The time in patience, wretched as it was ;
Till patience self, in her distempered sight,
Would seem a charm to which she had no right,
And trembling at the lip, and pale with fears,
She shook her head, and burst into fresh tears.
Old comforts now were not at her command :
The falcon reached in vain from off his stand ;
The flowers were not refreshed ; the very light,
The sunshine, seemed as if it shone at night ;

The least noise smote her like a sudden wound;
And did she hear but the remotest sound
Of song or instrument about the place,
She hid with both her hands her streaming face.
But worse to her than all (and oh! thought she,
That ever, ever such a worse could be!)
The sight of infant was, or child at play;
Then would she turn, and move her lips, and pray,
That heaven would take her, if it pleased, away.

I pass the meetings Paulo had with her:—
Calm were they in their outward character,
Or pallid efforts, rather, to suppress
The pangs within, that either's might be less;
And ended mostly with a passionate start
Of tears and kindness, when they came to part.
Thinner he grew, she thought, and pale with care;
" And I, 'twas I, that dashed his noble air!"

He saw her wasting, yet with placid shew;
And scarce could help exclaiming in his woe,
" O gentle creature, look not at me so !"

But Prince Giovanni, whom her wan distress
Had touched, of late, with a new tenderness,
Which to his fresh surprise did but appear
To wound her more than when he was severe,
Began, with other helps perhaps, to see
Strange things, and missed his brother's compan
What a convulsion was the first sensation !
Rage, wonder, misery, scorn, humiliation,
A self-love, struck as with a personal blow,
Gloomy revenge, a prospect full of woe,
All rushed upon him, like the sudden view
Of some new world, foreign to all he knew,
Where he had waked and found disease's visic
    true.

If any lingering hope that he was wrong,
Smoothed o'er him now and then, 'twas not so long.
Next night, as sullenly awake he lay,
Considering what to do.the approaching day,
He heard his wife say something in her sleep:—
He shook and listened;—she began to weep,
And moaning loudlier, seemed to shake her head,
Till all at once articulate, she said,
"He loves his brother yet—dear heaven, 'twas I—"
Then lower voiced—" only—*do* let me die."

The prince looked at her hastily;—no more;
He dresses, takes his sword, and through the door
Goes, like a spirit, in the morning air;—
His squire awaked attends; and they repair,
Silent as wonder, to his brother's room:—
*His* squire calls him up too; and forth they come.

The brothers meet,—Giovanni scarce in breath,
Yet firm and fierce, Paulo as pale as death.
" May I request, sir," said the prince, and frowned,
" Your ear a moment in the tilting ground ? "
" *There*, brother ?" answered Paulo, with an air
Surprised and shocked.  " Yes, *brother*," cried he,
    " there."
The word smote crushingly ; and paler still,
He bowed, and moved his lips, as waiting on his will.

Giovanni turned, and from the tower descending,
The squires, with looks of sad surprise, attending,
They issued forth in the moist-striking air,
And toward the tilt-yard crossed a planted square.
'Twas a fresh autumn dawn, vigorous and chill ;
The lightsome morning star was sparkling still,
Ere it turned in to heaven ; and far away
Appeared the streaky fingers of the day.

An opening in the trees took Paulo's eye,
As, with his brother, mutely he went by:
It was a glimpse of the tall wooded mound,
That screened Francesca's favorite spot of ground:
Massy and dark in the clear twilight stood,
As in a lingering sleep, the solemn wood;
And through the bowering arch, which led inside,
He almost fancied once, that he descried
A marble gleam, where the pavilion lay;—
Starting he turned, and looked another way.

Arrived, and the two squires withdrawn apart,
The prince spoke low, as with a labouring heart,
And said, " Before you answer what you can,
" I wish to tell you, as a gentleman,          •
" That what you may confess," (and as he spoke
His voice with breathless and pale passion broke)
" Will implicate no person known to you,
" More than disquiet in its sleep may do."

Paulo's heart bled; he waved his hand, and bent
His head a little in acknowledgment.

" Say then, sir, if you can," continued he,

" One word will do—you have not injured me :

" Tell me but so, and I shall bear the pain

" Of having asked a question I disdain;—

" But utter nothing, if not that one word;

" And meet me this :"—he stopped, and drew his
    sword.

Paulo seemed firmer grown from his despair ;
He drew a little back ; and with the air
Of one who would do well, not from a right
To be well thought of, but in guilt's despite,

" I am," said he, " I know,—'twas not so ever—

" But fight for it ! and with a brother ! Never."

" How !" with uplifted voice, exclaimed the other;

" The vile pretence! who asked you—with a *brother* ?

" Brother ! O traitor to the noble name

" Of Malatesta, I deny the claim.

" What ! wound it deepest? strike me to the core,
" Me, and the hopes which I can have no more,
" And then, as never Malatesta could,
" Shrink from the letting a few drops of blood ?"


" It is not so," cried Paulo, " 'tis not so ;
" But I would save you from a further woe."


" A further woe, recreant," retorted he :
" I know of none: yes, one there still may be:
" Save me the woe, save me the dire disgrace
" Of seeing one of an illustrious race
" Bearing about a heart, which feared no law,
" And a vile sword, which yet he dare not draw."


" Brother, dear brother !" Paulo cried, " nay, nay,
" I'll use the word no more;—but *peace*, I pray!
" You trample on a soul, sunk at your feet !"
" 'Tis false ;" exclaimed the prince ;. " 'tis a retreat

" To which you fly, when manly wrongs pursue,
" And fear the grave you bring a woman to."


A sudden start, yet not of pride or pain,
Paulo here gave; he seemed to rise again;
And taking off his cap without a word,
He drew, and kissed the crossed hilt of his sword,
Looking to heaven;—then with a steady brow,
Mild, yet not feeble, said, " I'm ready now."


" A noble word !" exclaimed the prince, and smot
Preparingly on earth his firming foot :—
The squires rushed in between, in their despair,
But both the princes told them to beware.


" Back, Gerard," cried Giovanni ; " I require
" No teacher here, but an observant squire."
" Back, Tristan," Paulo cried; fear not for me;
" All is not worst that so appears to thee.

"And here," said he, " a word."   The poor youth
    came,
Starting in sweeter tears to hear his name.
A whisper, and a charge there seemed to be,
Given to him kindly yet inflexibly :
Both squires then drew apart again, and stood
Mournfully both, each in his several mood,—
The one half sullen at these dreadful freaks,
The other with the tears streaming down both his
    cheeks.

The prince attacked with all his might and main,
Nor seemed the other slow to strike again ;
Yet as the fight grew warm, 'twas evident,
One fought to wound, the other to prevent :
Giovanni pressed, and pushed, and shifted aim,
And played his weapon like a tongue of flame ;
Paulo retired, and warded, turned on heel,
And led him, step by step, round like a wheel.

H

Sometimes indeed he feigned an angrier start,
But still relapsed, and played his former part.
" What!" cried Giovanni, who grew still more fierce,
" Fighting in sport? Playing your cart and tierce?"
" Not so, my prince," said Paulo; " have a care
" How you think so, or I shall wound you there."
He stamped, and watching as he spoke the word,
Drove, with his breast, full on his brother's sword.
'Twas done. He staggered, and in falling prest
Giovanni's foot with his right hand and breast:
Then on his elbow turned, and raising t'other,
He smiled, and said, " No fault of yours, my brother;
" An accident—a slip—the finishing one
" To errors by that poor old man begun.
" You'll not—you'll not"—his heart leaped on before,
And choked his utterance; but he smiled once more,
For, as his hand grew lax, he felt it prest;—
And so, his dim eyes sliding into rest,

He turned him round, and dropt with hiding head,
And, in that loosening drop, his spirit fled.


But noble passion touched Giovanni's soul;
He seemed to feel the clouds of habit roll
Away from him at once, with all their scorning;
And out he spoke in the clear air of morning :—
" By heaven, by heaven, and all the better part
" Of us poor creatures with a human heart,
" I trust we reap at last, as well as plough;—
" But there, meantime, my brother, liest thou;
" And, Paulo, thou wert the completest knight,
" That ever rode with banner to the fight;
" And thou wert the most beautiful to see,
" That ever came in press of chivalry;
" And of a sinful man  thou wert the best,
" That ever for his friend put spear in rest;
" And thou wert the most meek and cordial,
" That ever among ladies eat in hall;

" And thou wert still, for all that bosom gored,
" The kindest man, that ever struck with sword."

At this the words forsook his tongue ; and he,
Who scarcely had shed tears since infancy,
Felt his stern visage thrill, and meekly bowed
His head, and for his brother wept aloud.
The squires with glimmering tears,—Tristan, indeed
Heart-struck, and hardly able to proceed,—
Double their scarfs about the fatal wound,
And raise the body up to quit the ground.
Giovanni starts ; and motioning to take
The way they came, follows his brother back,
And having seen him laid upon the bed,
No further look he gave him, nor tear shed,
But went away, such as he used to be,
With looks of stately will, and calm austerity.

Tristan, who, when he was to make the best
Of something sad and not to be redressed,
Could shew a heart as firm as it was kind,
Now locked his tears up, and seemed all resigned,
And to Francesca's chamber took his way,
To tell her what his master bade him say.
He found her ladies up and down the stairs
Moving with noiseless caution, and in tears,
And that the sad news had before him got,
Though she herself, it seemed, yet knew it not.
The door, as tenderly as miser's purse,
Was opened to him by her aged nurse,
Who shaking her old head, and pressing close
Her withered lips to keep the tears that rose,
Made signs she guessed what 'twas he came about,
And so his arm squeezed gently, and went out.

The princess, who had passed a fearful night,
Toiling with dreams,—fright crowding upon fright,

Had missed her husband at that early hour,
And when she tried to rise, found she'd no power.
Yet as her body seemed to go, her mind
Felt, though in anguish still, strangely resigned ;
And moving not, nor weeping, mute she lay,
Wasting in patient gravity away.
The nurse sometime before with gentle creep
Had drawn the curtains, hoping she might sleep :
But suddenly she asked, though not with fear,
" Brangin, what bustle's that I seem to hear ?"
And the poor creature, who the news had heard,
Pretending to be busy, had just stirred
Something about the room, and answered not a word.

" Who's there?" said that sweet voice, kindly and
        clear,
Which in its stronger days was joy to hear :—
Its weakness now almost deprived the squire
Of his new firmness, but approaching nigher,

" Madam," said he, " 'tis I; one who may say,

" He loves his friends more than himself to-day;—

" Tristan."—She paused a little, and then said—

" Tristan—my friend, what noise thus haunts my
  head?

" Something I'm sure has happened—tell me what—

" I can bear all, though you may fancy not."

" Madam," replied the squire, " you are, I know,

" All sweetness—pardon me for saying so.

" My master bade me say then," resumed he,

" That he spoke firmly, when he told it me,—

" That I was also, madam, to your ear

" Firmly to speak, and you firmly to hear,—

" That he was forced this day, whether or no,

" To combat with the prince; and that although

" His noble brother was no fratricide,

" Yet in that fight, and on his sword,—he died."

" I understand,'' with firmness answered she;
More low in voice, but still composedly.
" Now, Tristan—faithful friend—leave me; and take
" This trifle here, and keep it for my sake."
So saying, from the curtains she put forth
Her thin white hand, that wore a ring of worth;
And he, with tears no longer to be kept
From quenching his heart's thirst, silently wept,
And kneeling took the ring, and touched her hand
To either streaming eye, with homage bland,
And looking on it once, gently up started,
And, in his reverent stillness, so departed.

Her favourite lady then with the old nurse
Returned, and fearing she must now be worse,
Gently withdrew the curtains, and looked in :—
O, who that feels one godlike spark within,
Shall say that earthly suffering cancels not frail sin!

There lay she praying, upwardly intent,
Like a fair statue on a monument,
With her two trembling hands together prest,
Palm against palm, and pointing from her breast.
She ceased, and turning slowly towards the wall,
They saw her tremble sharply, feet and all,—
Then suddenly be still.   Near more near
They bent with pale inquiry and close ear ;—
Her eyes were shut—no motion—not a breath—
The gentle sufferer was at peace in death.

I pass the grief that struck to every face,
And the mute anguish all about that place,
In which the silent people, here and there,
Went soft, as if she still could feel their care.
The gentle-tempered for a while forgot
Their own distress, or wept the common lot ;

The warmer, apter now to take offence,
Yet hushed as they rebuked, and wondered whence
Others at such a time could get their want of sense.


Fain would I haste indeed to finish all;
And so at once I reach the funeral.
Private 'twas fancied it must be, though some
Thought that her sire, the poor old duke, would come:
And some were wondering in their pity, whether
The lovers might not have one grave together.
Next day, however, from the palace gate
A blast of trumpets blew, like voice of fate;
And all in sable clad, forth came again
Of knights and squires the former sprightly train;
Gerard was next, and then a rank of friars;
And then, with heralds on each side, two squires,
The one of whom upon a cushion bore
The coroneted helm Prince Paulo wore,

His shield the other ;—then there was a space,
And in the middle, with a doubtful pace,
His horse succeeded, plumed and trapped in black,
Bearing the sword and banner on his back:
The noble creature, as in state he trod,
Appeared as if he missed his princely load;
And with back-rolling eye and lingering pride,
To hope his master still might come to ride.
Then Tristan, heedless of what passed around,
Rode by himself, with eyes upon the ground.
Then heralds in a row : and last of all
Appeared a hearse, hung with an ermined pall,
And bearing on its top, together set,
A prince's and princess's coronet.
Mutely they issued forth, black, slow, dejected,
Nor stopped within the walls, as most expected ;
But passed the gates—the bridge—the last abode,—
And towards Ravenna held their silent road.

The prince, it seems, struck since his brother's death,
With what he hinted with his dying breath,
And told by others now of all they knew,
Had instantly determined what to do;
And from a mingled feeling, which he strove
To hide no longer from his taught self-love,
Of sorrow, shame, resentment, and a sense
Of justice owing to that first offence,
Had, on the day preceding, written word
To the old duke of all that had occurred.
" And though I shall not," (so concluded he)
" Otherwise touch thine age's misery,
" Yet as I would that both one grave should hide,
" Which can, and must not be, where I reside,
" 'Tis fit, though all have something to deplore,
" That he, who joined them once, should keep to
part no more."

The wretched father, who, when he had read
This letter, felt it wither his grey head,
And ever since had paced his room about,
Trembling, and at the windows looking out,
Had given such orders, as he well could frame,
To meet devoutly whatsoever came ;
And as the news immediately took flight,
Few in Ravenna went to sleep that night,
But talked the business over, and reviewed
All that they knew of her, the fair and good ;
And so with wondering sorrow the next day
Waited till they should see that sad array.

The days were then at close of autumn,—still,
A little rainy, and towards night-fall chill;
There was a fitful, moaning air abroad;
And ever and anon, over the road,
The last few leaves came fluttering from the trees,
Whose trunks now thronged to sight, in dark varieties.

The  people, who from reverence kept at home,
Listened till afternoon to hear them come;
And hour on hour went by, and nought was heard
But some chance horseman, or the wind that stirred,
Till towards the vesper hour; and then, 'twas said
Some heard a voice, which seemed as if it read;
And others said, that they could hear a sound
Of many horses trampling the moist ground.
Still nothing came,—till on a sudden, just
As the wind opened in a rising gust,
A voice of chanting rose, and as it spread,
They plainly heard the anthem for the dead.
It was the choristers who went to meet
The train, and now were entering the first street.
Then turned aside that city, young and old,
And in their lifted hands the gushing sorrow rolled.

But of the older people, few could bear
To keep the window, when the train drew near;

## 111

And all felt double tenderness to see
The bier approaching, slow and steadily,
On which those two in senseless coldness lay,
Who but a few short months—it seemed a day,
Had left their walls, lovely in form and mind,
In sunny manhood he,—she first of womankind.

They say that when Duke Guido saw them come,
He clasped his hands, and looking round the room,
Lost his old wits for ever.  From the morrow
None saw him after.  But no more of sorrow.
On that same night, those lovers silently
Were buried in one grave, under a tree.
There side by side, and hand in hand, they lay
In the green ground:—and on fine nights in May
Young hearts betrothed used to go there to pray.

THE END.

Printed in Great Britain
by Amazon

13075680R00079